VIEWFINDER

poems by

Stephanie Blair Mitchell

Finishing Line Press
Georgetown, Kentucky

VIEWFINDER

Copyright © 2025 by Stephanie Blair Mitchell
ISBN 979-8-89990-258-1 First Edition
All rights reserved under International and Pan-American Copyright Conventions. No part of this book may be reproduced in any manner whatsoever without written permission from the publisher, except in the case of brief quotations embodied in critical articles and reviews.

Publisher: Leah Huete de Maines
Editor: Christen Kincaid
Cover Art: Stephanie Blair Mitchell
Author Photo: Stephanie Blair Mitchell
Cover Design: Elizabeth Maines McCleavy

Order online: www.finishinglinepress.com
also available on amazon.com

Author inquiries and mail orders:
Finishing Line Press
PO Box 1626
Georgetown, Kentucky 40324
USA

Contents

Statement x

View from the Window at Le Gras, c. 1826 1
Boulevard du Temple, 1838 3
Fallen Child, 1989 5
Town of Le Brusc, France, 1976 9
Edith in Panama, Ocher, 2005 10
Pomona, 1872 12
Migrant Mother, 1936 14
Jessie Tarbox Beals, 1904 16
Saigon Execution, 1968 19
Lee Miller, Munich, Germany, 1945 20
Mahatma Gandhi Spinning, 1946 23
Santa Maria della Salute in Palazzo Bedroom, Venice, Italy, 2006 24
Gavin Coal Power Plant, Cheshire, Ohio, 2003 27
Parking Site 1, 2007 28
Early Impressions 30
Sonnet to Salt 32
Mary Saba 34
Pool Shovel 37
You're Muted 38
Mental Picture 39
Art of the Portrait 40
My People 41
Darkroom Dedication 42
Silent Shutter 43

Acknowledgments 44

For Solveig and Lucian

Statement

Photography and poetry—two art forms known for distillation and acute observations—combine in this volume.

Photography has encircled me since my earliest moments. My father, an art professor at the local college, maintained a home darkroom and by the time I was ten, taught me black and white film developing and printing. When I was in middle school, he guided me through science fair projects that explored pinhole cameras and Sabatier Effect, the darkroom photographic phenomenon that reverses image tones. When I reached high school, he encouraged my interest taking me to a photo trade show in Baltimore where I purchased my first camera—a Nikon EM with a 50mm lens. And after college, he took great pleasure when I landed my first job working at a daily newspaper.

Today, I am still a photographer and have devoted decades to image making, sampling most every camera format and following photographic advances from black and white and color film to DSLR and mirrorless technologies. Now in my fifties, I pause to consider photography—its origins, the legendary artists and images that drew me to the craft, the experience of the practitioner, my unique story, and the shifting role of the profession in the world.

Since my youth, poetry has traveled a parallel path of significance. A series of librarians, teachers, professors, and once again, my father nurtured an appreciation of the verse. Reciting, memorizing, and studying ancient and contemporary poets was a source of solace and delight. When I became a mother, I often reached for poetry books as bedtime reading to my children. My daughter, a talented writer and poet, reinforced my interest. An echo of the link between my father and me, my daughter and I have shared our affection for poetry by attending author events and poetry readings. My son, who has a gift for numbers and patterns, helped me resolve the structure and shape of certain poems within this collection. Most significantly, my children posed the writing challenge that led to the making of this book.

Both photography and poetry attend to light and space, abstract time and reality, and stir sensations and emotions. As I began writing these verses, their interplay, the pairing of photography and poetry, could not be more natural and enticing.

This collection begins with the oldest surviving image, the heliograph *View from the Window at Le Gras*, and the first known image of a person, the daguerreotype *Boulevard du Temple*, moves through images of particular personal resonance, and pulls in photographs from my family archive.

May fellow viewfinders take pleasure in this reverie of the art of photography.

Joseph Nicéphore Niépce
View from the Window at Le Gras, c. 1826
Heliograph
6.4 x 8 inches (16.2 x 20.2 cm)

View from the Window at Le Gras, c. 1826

Escher sketch
in binary light and shadow

Sun writing
lavender oil and petroleum
on a pewter plate

The first 'decisive moment'
lasted eight hours

It transpired in 1826
or 1827—
an odd uncertainty
for a medium
rooted in recording
precise fractions of time

A wash house, a pigeon house
a bake house roof
and an orchard pear tree

The work room window
frames the modest View

Niépce's original
is eclipsed by Daguerre

For nearly fifty years
it slips into obscurity.

Louis Jacques Mandé Daguerre
Boulevard du Temple, 1838
Daguerreotype
5 x 6 inches (13 x 16 cm)

Boulevard du Temple, 1838

Historian resurrects the
blistered and battered frame
once cherished, then overlooked—

daguerreotype—
named immodestly
after its creator

part art part science
image bestowed
on King Ludwig I of Bavaria

conspiracy between copper sheets
silver and mercury fumes
set with sodium thiosulfate

spirited scene
stripped to its architecture
and tree-lined street

unknown and unaware
a nameless pair
persists perpetually

their stillness
their moment of pause
immortal

man stands
before ghostly
bootblack.

Fallen Child, 1989

It was Thanksgiving 1992
when my family stumbled
upon the Houk Friedman Gallery

Sally Mann's world,
judged "controversial" by critics,
mirrored my childhood

My artist parents
saw no shame in
naked bodies

encouraged night swimming and
summer days of make-believe
in Maryland backwoods and waters.

Immediate Family
Our parallel wild brood
with a boy and two girls—

Chris, the eldest,
was Emmett, leading the pack,
carving a path upstream

Jennie was Jessie,
with all her sass
and latent sexuality

And I, the youngest,
saw myself,
slight yet
steady and strong,
reflected in Virginia.

Bee stings, baby dolls,
blood stains, bite marks,
scratches, and swollen eyes

early drama and trauma
through a view camera
naturally conveyed.

Landscapes
familiar in their
fabrics and notions

pulled me to the craft
teetering, tumbling
toward certainty.

Mann possessed
Cameron's touch
yet darkly elegiac—

Look at the cradle
without seeing the grave,
she dared.

"Fallen Child"
curly locks splayed
her back marred by needles

Virginia in free fall.

Sally Mann
Fallen Child, 1989
Silver gelatin print
8 x 10 inches (20.3 x 25.4 cm)
Edition of 25
© Sally Mann
Courtesy of the artist and Gagosian

Martine Franck
Town of Le Brusc, France, 1976
Gelatin silver print
12 x 18 inches (30.48 cm x 45.72 cm)
© Martine Franck/Magnum Photos

Town of Le Brusc, France, 1976

"Martine, I want to come
see your contact sheets,"
said Henri to Ms. Franck

Thirty years her senior
the pioneer of street photography
made his opening move.

Despite Henri's long shadow
Martine carved distinct
forms and light

Layered and balanced
her frames spoke
dialect of distinction

Modest by nature
photography her voice
every portrait a conversation

"In photography,
I found a language
that suits me."

Artists, authors, elderly, the poor
she sought small intimacies
soulful compositions

Tiptoed across boundaries
forgetting herself
to receive others

She ran while changing
film to frame
sunbathers poolside at Le Brusc

Basking, stretching, soaking
hammock reflection
in repose.

Edith in Panama, Ocher, 2005

Emmet Gowin, an artist
whose creations evolved
untold dimensions

Circle frame, secret keyhole
4x5 lens on an 8x10 body
vignettes, telescopes, focuses

your family photos
recall shared
childhood memories.

Edith, your model and muse,
encircled in light
shrouded and sheer

screens and fabrics
of diaphanous flow
exposed her form

pictured from behind
female embrace
we enter her space.

Your photographs like family stories
never tire, bear repeating, circling back
eggs held in a contorted clasp

Nocturnal moths
ephemera on a wing
lands the closing verse.

Emmet Gowin
Edith in Panama, ocher, 2005
Salt print on handmade Twinrocker paper
15.9 x 10.5 inches (40.3 x 26.7 cm)
© Emmet and Edith Gowin
Courtesy of Pace Gallery, New York

Pomona, 1872

A month before
my father's demise

from his hospice bed
brain diminished from cancer

we discovered
black and white page

of an angel
and mountain nymph

mythological depiction
from Freshwater, Isle of Wight.

The book,
a birthday gift,

given months before
signed, Love Dad

(fellow photographer)
dated 5.5.99

his signature strokes
characteristically strong

mountainous ridges
marked the M.

Words were waning,
all but disappeared

still his artistic dexterity
sustained, sketching

graphite delineations
soft focus dream portraitist

He drew your details
dazzled in your light and dark.

Julia Margaret Cameron
Pomona, 1872
Albumen silver print
19.6 x 14.8 inches (49.7 x 37.4 cm)

Migrant Mother, 1936

Few words
were exchanged
along highway 101
when Florence
drew back the curtain
fixed her eyes
on distant horizons

Her thumb
caught the corner
muddled the feeling
and was promptly
retouched

Erased to enhance—
a shocking revelation
to the documentary purist

Dorothea seized
seven frames
and with one
entered our
eternal consciousness

For forty years
her identity was
obscured and shrouded

Mythical migrant mother
shouldered our collective
struggles and despairs.

Dorothea Lange
Migrant Mother, 1936
Gelatin silver print
11.1 × 8.6 inches (28.3 × 21.8 cm)

Jessie Tarbox Beals, 1904

First female photojournalist climbs great heights
new angles and perspectives she reveals

Atop trees, trains, telephone poles she delights
flying from hot air balloons to automobiles

Buffalo Burdick murder trial ignites
she scoops the nation and all the newsreels

Louisiana Purchase Exposition highlights
Bagabos headhunters with beaded bags eating meals

Bedouin women and sword dancing incites
Ainu man from Japan and Ferris wheels

Despite all the distinctive and uncommon sights
someone points their camera at Jessie Tarbox Beals.

Unidentified Artist
Untitled (Jessie Tarbox Beals preparing to take photograph atop high ladder, main entrance of the Austrian Pavilion, 1904 St. Louis World's Fair), Harvard Art Museums/Fogg Museum, Transfer from the Carpenter Center for the Visual Arts, Photo © President and Fellow of Harvard College, 2.2002.3162
6.8 x 4.8 in. (17.2 x 12.2 cm)

Eddie Adams
Saigon Execution, 1968
Associated Press
Gelatin silver print
8 x 10 inches (20.3 x 25.4 cm)

Saigon Execution, 1968

I am not content with content—
somewhere in the
corporate catchphrase
the craft is lost

Photography—
simple shutter
split second
four-edged frame

Adams, Ut, Lange—
their photographs shook
the course of culture
recovered us from war, the farmers' plight

There is magic in the moment—
moments inspire movements—
History is not changed
by being content.

Lee Miller, Munich, Germany, 1945

What was going through
your head?

Fresh from the fields
of Dachau
filth and
human remains
soiling your skin

when you slipped into
der Führer's bath
boots planted aside

You couldn't have known
of his demise
that exact day
by suicide.

Was it victory or anger?
Was it repulsion or fatigue
as you rinsed away
the film of depravity?

Lee Miller with David E Scherman
Lee Miller in Hitler's bathtub, Hitler's apartment,
16 Prinzregentenplatz, Munich, Germany 1945
Gelatin silver print
9 x 9 inches (23 x 23 cm)
© Lee Miller Archives, England 2024. All rights reserved. leemiller.co.uk

Margaret Bourke-White
Mahatma Gandhi Spinning, 1946
Gelatin silver print
14.6 × 19.5 inches (37.1 × 49.5 cm)
The *LIFE* Picture Collection/Shutterstock

Mahatma Gandhi Spinning, 1946

Sitting silent, Gandhi and spinning circle
symbol of independence, guiding circle

Tool of political emancipation, charkha
ancient work ethics, self-reliant revolving circle

Non-violent protest, centered on India's flag.
Simple wooden spindles turn, liberating circle

Twenty-four spokes and spindle spun yarn,
wheel of unity and law, freeing circle.

Challenged by dim light, Margaret Bourke-White
aims her lens, opens her aperture, widening circle.

"To throw my whole self into recording and attempting to understand
…an inner serenity as a kind of balance," centering circle.

Movement, progress, each revolution, each turn, each frame
perpetual change, capturing truth, exposing injustice, cycling circle.

Silvered diopter, odd number of blades, frames the scene,
reflecting, refracting, mirroring circle.

My dear photo mentor once declared the triangle
to be the strongest form, I submitted, it is the uniting circle.

Santa Maria della Salute in Palazzo Bedroom, Venice, Italy, 2006

First revelations are homegrown
from your son Brady's bedroom
castles and dinosaurs collide
with a street scene in Brookline

Curators marvel at your
childlike fascination
and applaud
your novel projections

The world is your playground
from Cuba
to New York, Italy, and France
grand displays cast onto interior places

Creating darkened chambers
tape and plastic
transform rooms into cameras
canvases are inner outer spaces

With patient exposures
street scenes and activity dissolve
there are no people
in your crisscrossed worlds

Synchronized diptych
single view of two views
overlay of
newborn dimension.

Abelardo Morell
Santa Maria della Salute in Palazzo Bedroom, Venice, Italy, 2006
Large-format archival pigment print
37.8 x 29.8 in (95.9 x 75.6 cm)
© 2024 Abelardo Morell
Image courtesy of Krakow Witkin Gallery, Boston

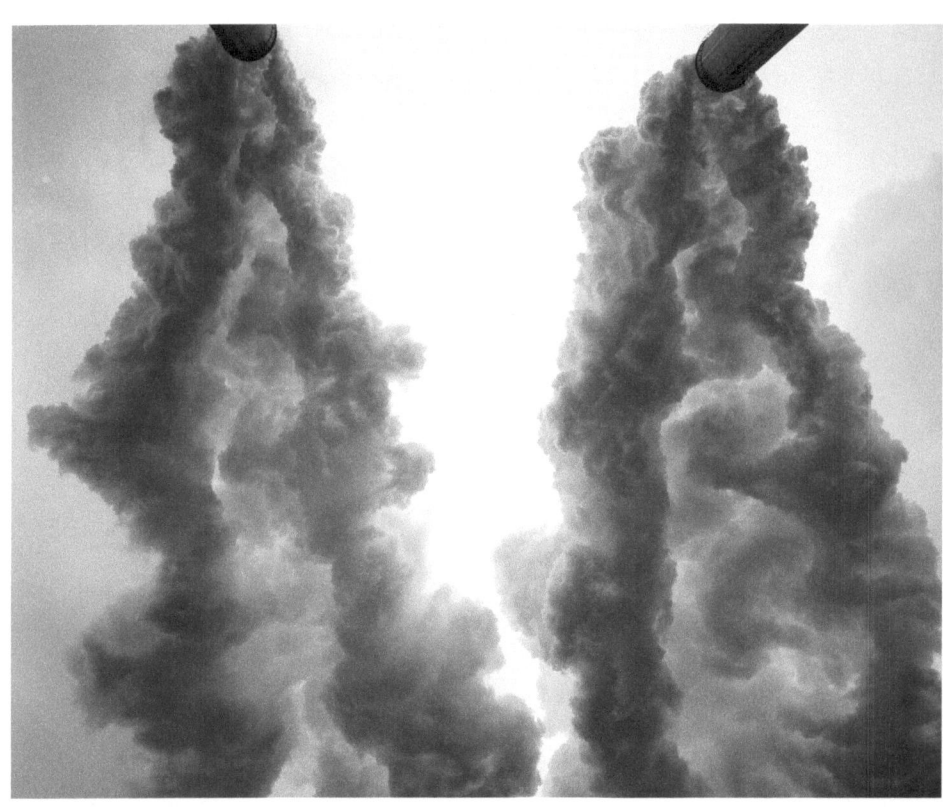

Mitch Epstein
Gavin Coal Power Plant, Cheshire, Ohio, 2003
© Black River Productions, Ltd. / Mitch Epstein.
Courtesy of Sikkema Jenkins & Co., New York.
Used with permission. All rights reserved.

Gavin Coal Power Plant, Cheshire, Ohio, 2003

Twin towers imprint
On American psyche

Projects of
American Power

"Human conquest
Of nature at any cost"

Epstein warns
Of contaminated waters

Of acid air plumes
Dissolving township

A country fights
Against its own interest—

Two stacks spew smoke
A self-inflicted wound.

Parking Site 1, 2007

Supervisions
watchful eye of surveillance
a new way of seeing

Aerial views
reveal repetitions
precision pixel puzzles

Multiple frames
stitch together
elevate to a single image

Beach sands crowded with footprints
ocean waters ripple with activity
invisible evidence of human passage

Rows of trees cast elongated shadows
that lengthen and shift
reflecting the sun's movement

Topsy turvy time riddles
motion and chaos
collapse to stillness.

Andreas Gefeller
Untitled (Parking Site 1)
Düsseldorf, 2007
From the series Supervisions
Color print
66.9 x 87.8 inches (170 x 223 cm)
© Andreas Gefeller

Early Impressions

"The first thing
you saw
in this entire world
was a Nikon,"

said my father's best friend,
a physics professor
and part time photographer.

He photographed
my homebirth
on a dead-end street
in Baltimore.

He shared this with me
for the first time
at my father's memorial.

WWII camoufleur
turned artist
and educator

My father's film
had reached
its final frame.

I was twenty-five,
a photographer,
and my camera
was a Nikon.

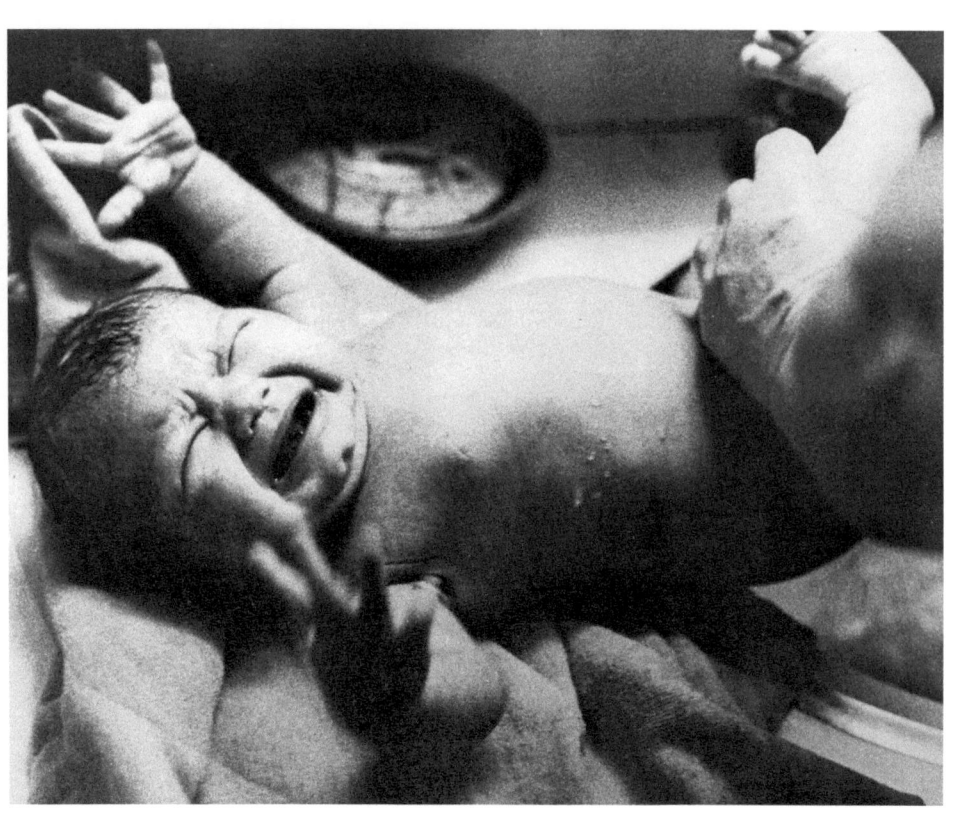

Bill Pelham
Home Birth, 1974
Gelatin silver print
8 x 10 inches (20.3 x 25.4 cm)
© Bill Pelham

Sonnet to Salt

Under (your nose) World, Holzman Gallery
My father's work took on new shape
Science met art through photomicrography
Salt crystals became a mountain scape

It was the summer of '85
we printed invitations for the show
The photographer in me came alive
in the darkroom red lights aglow

Ten years later at Salt Magazine
following my dream to study firsthand
In Portland, Maine, I photographed the scene
of air of water of people of land

Thousands of uses mysteriously,
essential element of convergency.

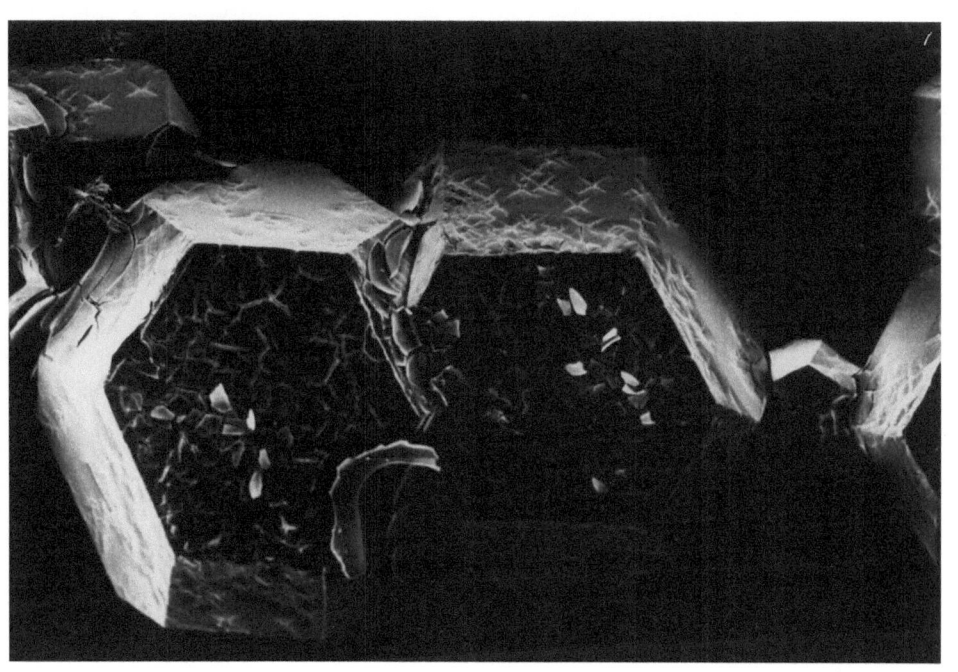

John Blair Mitchell
Salt, 1985
Gelatin silver print
8 x 12 inches (20.3 x 30.9 cm)
© John Blair Mitchell

Mary Saba

Girl framed
Contained

While
Boys play
Splay

Viewfinder
Sees her

37th frame
Chance
Dance

From Ethiopia
To Maine
Altered state
New terrain

Shifting lives
Fresh view
"Time and place
Change you."

Stephanie Blair Mitchell
Mary Saba, 1995
Gelatin silver print
8 x 12 inches (20.3 x 30.9 cm)
Courtesy of Salt Institute for Documentary Studies
© Stephanie Blair Mitchell

Margaret Mitchell
Pool Shovel, 2000
Color print
8 x 12 inches (20.3 x 30.9 cm)
© Margaret Mitchell

Pool Shovel
after Terrance Hayes

Blue bowl of coarse cement that the
neighborhood skaters peer at with saddest
expressions, imagining the part
of the year when the water is
drained and where
like archeological remains the
peeling paint and dirt
recall past summers, says
the memories of our childish delights, it
speaks of swimming, squealing, summersaulting to
midnight skinny dipping, to the
fall, when the surrounding trees shed their leaves and seeds,
the winter incapsulates in
ice and decays, making way for the
spring peepers and toad eggs in clumps and rows, flowers
color the surrounding garden above
as my brother and I scoop the
primordial sludge at the base of the grave.

You're Muted

It is a strange time to be an introvert
when everyone clamors for the mic

It is not shyness
anxiety
nothing to say

I prefer silence
observe the details
sway the in-between

Tacit movement
through space

Ears soften
eyes attend to
form and shadows

Cameras capture
the unutterable.

Mental Picture

Primordial beast spawns
spikey exoskeleton
stirs waters above

streamline ripple hints
to its one ton
flip across
aerobic realms
along the Kennebec River

silent satellites glide
past stagnant sea
waiting, scanning
a tiny, dust speck
sent across the celestial water
a streak of light

sturgeon splashes—
we squeal with delight
not a camera in sight.

Art of the Portrait

It's a delicate proposition
asking a person

to face *their* face
a subject is sometimes sensitive

Eyes sunken or wrinkled
belly swollen or chin crinkled

hair gone gray or fallen away
nose negativity—a classic cliche

The photographer masks
science while striding together

fluid dance
mirrored fidelity

working in tandem
duet in portrayal.

My People

I see you glide
through the crowd
your unique gait

Invisible
sliding to the best spot
worn canvas bag
slumped over shoulder.

Dressed to blend
black shirt
masks discrete strap
brand obscured
with gaffers' tape

Years of observation
searching for edges
leaves the final clue
telltale eyes askew.

Darkroom Dedication

Darkroom illuminates with red light enlarger
casts the negative imprint while trays
of liquid magically reveal black and
white positive patterns shortstop seizes slippery
developer marking time by swirling seconds
hours accelerate until night develops dawn.

Silent Shutter

The symphony of clacks and whirls
has been in rapid decrescendo

Clumsy fumbling of the film holder
4x5 slide removed and then replaced
a single snap

Threaded 120 film slithers
spool and leader
rolls and advances

Rapid fire staccato of the 35mm
each model humming a different pitch

To the trained ear the brand is revealed
a subtle difference to the shutter sound
Nikon, Canon—the discreet Leica hush

Light refraction and lens physics
now invisible, instantaneous
fade from whisper to whispered

I mourn the moment in-between, the Intermission,
time to guess, hope, contemplate
what may have been captured or missed

Silver has long ago faded from view
making way for bits and pixels
yet the craft endures, the resolution the solution

Signature style cannot hide
inevitable is the individual
fingerprint on glass.

Acknowledgments

I am grateful to the editors of *Harvard Review Online* for publishing "View from the Window at Le Gras, c. 1826."

My sincere thanks to the early readers and editors that include poets Alec Solomita, Chloe Garcia Roberts, Heather Nelson, and Ralph Pennel. Their encouragement and advice have been critical to this manuscript.

Deep gratitude to the celebrated photographers Sally Mann, Emmet Gowin, Abelardo Morell, Mitch Epstein, and Andreas Gefeller, who generously shared their works with me for publication and who have inspired me and countless photographers with their images, to the photo collectives and archives at Magnum Photos, Harvard Art Museums, Lee Miller Archive, and *LIFE* Picture Collection/Shutterstock, that granted permission for the photographs of Martine Franck, Jessie Tarbox Beals, Lee Miller, and Margaret Bourke-White, to the works by Joseph Nicéphore Niépce, Louis Jacques Mandé Daguerre, Julia Margaret Cameron, Dorothea Lange, and Eddie Adams, now in the public domain, and to Salt Institute for Documentary Studies, the children of Bill Pelham, and my mother and artist Margaret Mitchell, who provided the personal family photographs.

"Pool Shovel," the golden shovel poem, is based on a line from "In the saddest part of the story the brother goes" in *American Sonnets for My Past and Future Assassin* by Terrance Hayes, the creator of the golden shovel form. My daughter and I had the privilege of hearing him recite the poem at a bookstore event, which sparked the inspiration for this poem.

I have studied with and worked alongside the most talented photographers from my days at Wellesley College, *Salt Magazine, Boston Herald,* and Harvard University. The camaraderie and lessons learned from my fellow photographers are among the most valuable that I carry with me to every assignment and are reflected in these pages of poetry.

Finally, I am eternally thankful to my dear family and friends who have supported me throughout this project, most especially my mother Margaret; my siblings Peter, Chris, and Jennie; my husband Andrew; my stepdaughter Autumn; and my children Solveig and Lucian—my light and loves.

Stephanie Blair Mitchell is Director of Photography at Harvard University where she has worked for over twenty-five years. A Baltimore native, she received her B.A. with honors from Wellesley College, studied photography at the Salt Institute for Documentary Studies, attended the Eddie Adams Workshop, and earned her master's degree in Studio Arts and Film from Harvard Extension School.

In the course of her work at Harvard, she has photographed seven Harvard Presidents, countless professors, staff, and students within the community, traveled internationally on assignments, and documented numerous notable figures during their visits to campus.

Her photographs have been selected for exhibitions curated by the National Press Photographers Association and the Cambridge Art Association, awarded recognition from the Boston Press Photographers Association Pictures of the Year Contest, and appeared in publications including *The New York Times, Washington Post, Boston Globe, Guardian, Irish Times, Der Spiegel,* and *Time Magazine.*

Stephanie lives with her family in Cambridge, Massachusetts. *Viewfinder* is her debut poetry book.

To learn more about the author, visit www.stephaniemitchell.com.

www.ingramcontent.com/pod-product-compliance
Lightning Source LLC
Chambersburg PA
CBHW042311150426
43198CB00006B/116